The Jewish Sabbath

A Crowell Holiday Book

The Jewish Sabbath

BY MOLLY CONE *Illustrated by Ellen Raskin*

THOMAS Y. CROWELL COMPANY • NEW YORK

CROWELL HOLIDAY BOOKS

Edited by Susan Bartlett Weber

Copyright © 1966 by Molly Cone
Illustrations copyright © 1966 by Ellen Raskin
All rights reserved. No part of this book may
be reproduced in any form, except by a reviewer,
without the permission of the publisher.
Manufactured in the United States of America.
Library of Congress Catalog Card No. 65-27292
Published in Canada by Fitzhenry & Whiteside Limited, Toronto
ISBN 0-690-46111-9
0-690-46112-7 (LB)
2 3 4 5 6 7 8 9 10

The Jewish Sabbath

Chicken soup means *Sabbath* to many Jewish children, for the Sabbath dinner in a Jewish home often begins with chicken soup. With chicken soup and blessings. First the blessings, then the soup, and after that, there are other good things to eat in honor of the Sabbath.

The Sabbath is a special day to the Jewish people. From the moment it begins at sunset on Friday evening, to the moment it ends at sunset on Saturday evening, it has a special feeling.

Perhaps this is because the Sabbath is a holiday. But it is different from all the other holidays, too. It is a Day of Rest.

The name *Sabbath* goes back to the beginning of the world as the Old Testament of the Bible tells it. God created the world in six days and on the seventh he rested. The seventh day was called the Sabbath. Sabbath comes from a Hebrew word, *Shabbat.* It means *rest.*

Sunday is the Sabbath to most Christians today. But Saturday has always been the Sabbath to the Jewish people. It is the oldest holiday they celebrate.

The keeping of the Sabbath is also a *law* to the Jewish people. It is an important part of their Torah. Torah is what Jewish people call all the learning they live by.

On the Jewish Sabbath, it is against the law to mourn. And against the law to worry. And against the law to *work*.

And how this law came to be is the story of the Sabbath.

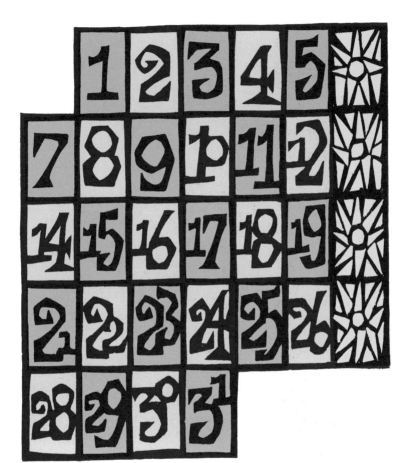

A long, long time ago, a people speaking Hebrew came to live in the land of Egypt. They came with great joy, for Joseph, one of their tribesmen, was already there. He was loved and respected by all the Egyptian people, and honored by their Pharaoh. Joseph's people, the Jews, lived there happily for many years.

Another Pharaoh rose to rule in Egypt. He did not like the strangers in his land. He set tasks for them. He set them to making bricks to build cities. And the harder they worked, the more work he gave them to do.

A lake cannot give water and never be refilled. A field cannot grow grain and never lie fallow. A person cannot work and never be refreshed. The lake becomes a dry bed. The field, barren ground. And the man — a slave.

The Jews became slaves in Egypt.

With God's help, Moses led them out
of the land of Egypt. The Bible tells how
God looked after them. It tells how He
gave them the Ten Commandments as
the law for free people to live by.

And in the Fourth Commandment was the secret of making freedom a part of their lives.

The Fourth Commandment said:

Remember the Sabbath day and keep it holy. Six days you shall labor and do all your work, but the seventh day is the Sabbath. On it you shall do no manner of work; not you, nor your son, nor your daughter, nor your servants, nor the animals in your house, nor the stranger within your gates. For in six days the Lord made heaven and earth and sea, and all that is in them, and He rested on the seventh day. . . .

The Jewish people made this Fourth Commandment their way of life. Because it was God's way. Like God, they did their work in six days. Like God, they rested on the seventh. Their animals who worked in the fields rested, too.

In ancient Palestine, a trumpet was blown to remind everyone to stop work for the Sabbath. Just before the sun went down, candles were lit to shine for the Sabbath.

To guard the right of rest, no work at all was allowed on the Sabbath day. No picking up sticks, no lighting of fires, no cooking. No working in stores, fields, or homes. It was against the law to do *any kind* of work on the Sabbath.

Most poor people ate only dark bread all the week long. But on the Sabbath, rich and poor alike ate white bread to honor the Sabbath. The bread was braided or twisted. A special napkin was laid over it. Like the candles, the Sabbath loaf became a symbol of the Day of Rest.

The Sabbath dinner was the finest of the week. Fish was chopped and spiced. Dough was rolled out thin and cut into fine noodles. The fattest chicken went into the soup.

In every Jewish house, the whole family gathered together for the Sabbath. No matter how poor a man was, nor how hard his workaday life, on the Sabbath he was a king in his home.

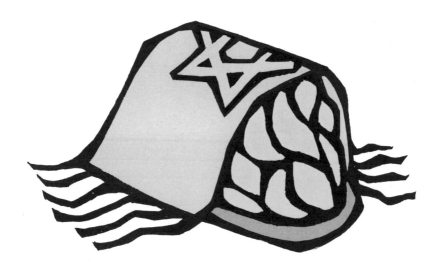

The Sabbath was a day of rest for a person *inside* himself too. In very early times, it was a day of study. Every town and village built a synagogue, a house of study. Jews would go every Sabbath to read the Torah and talk about its meanings.

The Sabbath became the very heart of Judaism, the Jewish religion.

Once there was a king who outlawed the Sabbath. All the Jews in his kingdom were ordered to bow down to idols. The

Hanukkah story tells how many of these Jews chose to die rather than to give up the Sabbath.

Hundreds of years later, in the Middle Ages, other rulers turned against people who were not Christians. But the Jews held on to their Sabbath. A poet wrote a poem about this.

In the poem, an evil witch put a spell on a handsome prince. The prince turned into an ugly dog. People ran away from him in fright. But the witch's evil spell did not hold on the Sabbath. Once a week, the ugly dog became a prince again!

The poem was not really a fairy tale, for every Jew felt like that ugly dog in those days. Only on the Sabbath, in his own home, did he feel like himself again. The Sabbath feeling kept his hope alive.

A story is told about a rich Persian who loved all manner of good things.

Passing a Jewish home on a Friday night, he smelled a delicious smell. He knocked at the door and asked what was cooking on the stove.

He took the recipe home to his wife. And she made the same kind of soup for him.

When it was done, the rich man sniffed at it. "This is not the same!" he said. He wondered if he had left something out of the recipe.

The next Friday afternoon, he again stopped at the Jewish house. As the door opened, the delicious smell tickled his nose. With great care he got the *exact* recipe for what was cooking on the stove.

Again his wife cooked the same thing for him, exactly the same way.

"Bah!" said the Persian, sniffing into the pot. "This is not the same at all!"

"The Jew is playing a trick on you!" the wife said angrily. "There must be a secret seasoning!"

The next Friday, after sundown, the Persian pounded loudly at the door of the Jew's house.

"Tell me, what is it that makes everything smell so good in this house every Friday night?" he demanded.

The Jew looked about his small home. The Sabbath candles spread their light over the dinner table. The Sabbath loaves lay ready under their napkin cover. A cup of wine stood by.

As it was every Sabbath at this time, all work had been put away. Food for the next day had been prepared. The windows sparkled; the floor was swept clean. His wife and children sat at the table with the glow of the Sabbath on their faces. It was true — a delicious aroma seemed to fill the house.

"You have a secret seasoning!" the Persian accused. "What is it?"

The Jew smiled. "The Sabbath itself is the seasoning that makes everything taste so good," he said.

Today, though many Sabbath customs have changed since ancient times, the Sabbath feeling is still the same.

In many Jewish homes the table is laid with a fine cloth on Friday night. Sabbath dinner is the best of the week.

Just before the sun goes down, the mother of the family lights the Sabbath candles. Softly, she says the blessing over them.

Then the father picks up the cup of wine and recites the special blessing over it. The wine is for the joy of the Sabbath.

Next a Sabbath loaf is passed around. The father says the blessing and all eat a bit of the bread.

The blessings are recited in Hebrew. They are thank-yous to God. They thank Him for the Torah. They thank Him for the Sabbath of Rest, and for life and home and family and the good food on the table.

"Good Sabbath!" is what everyone says after the blessings are recited. Or *"Shabbat Shalom,"* which means "Sabbath Peace to You." Then everyone eats the chicken soup and all the other good things made to celebrate the Sabbath.

All over the world, Jewish families begin the celebration of the Sabbath on Friday night. Many go to their synagogues and temples before dinner. Others go after dinner. Some go again on Saturday morning. In a Jewish home, on the Sabbath day, the whole house is at rest.

Some people rest by closing their eyes and thinking. Some people rest by walking, or visiting, or reading, or playing. Rest means being free to just *be.*

A person thinks a little bigger on the Sabbath. A person stands a little taller on the Sabbath. A person is a *person* on the Sabbath.

When three stars are seen in the sky on Saturday night, the Sabbath Day is ended. In many Jewish homes, good-bye to the

Day of Rest is said with blessings, too.

A wine cup is filled until it runs over. "May the coming week overflow with goodness like the wine in the cup," the head of the family says.

A box of spices is passed around. The good spice smell reminds everyone of the sweetness of the Sabbath just passed. Some who take a big sniff say they can even smell the Sabbath to come.

A last farewell is made over a lighted candle. It is a special candle of twisted strands. It is called a *Havdalah* candle.

Havdalah means "separation." The Havdalah blessings separate the holiday from the weekday.

The dusk has turned to darkness. The Sabbath is over. But its goodness is remembered all through the week — like chicken soup with blessings.

About the Author

Molly Cone has written numerous books for boys and girls of all ages. She brings to the writing of *The Jewish Sabbath* a deep interest in Jewish lore and a gift for clear storytelling.

Mrs. Cone has been writing since she was a student at the University of Washington. She and her husband and children make their home in Seattle, where they enjoy an active Northwest life.

About the Illustrator

Ellen Raskin is a well-known illustrator and designer of books and book jackets. She has received awards for her work from the Art Directors' Club of New York, the Society of Illustrators, and the American Institute of Graphic Arts.

Miss Raskin was born in Milwaukee, Wisconsin, and majored in art at the University of Wisconsin. She enjoys music and composes songs for the harpsichord and piano. She lives in New York City.

ENF   Cone, Molly
296.4   The Jewish Sabbath.
CON

MAHS01337

DATE			
FEB 7	NOV 23		
NOV 3			
		NOV 25	